DATE DUE

OC 21 03	MY 03 '07	APR 0 3 '09	OCT 1 9 '11
OC 04 04	OC 29 '07	APR 1 6 '09	
NO 17 '04	DE 17 '07	APR 2 9 '09	
DE 17 '04	JA 16	DEC 0 1 '09	
DE 21 '04	JAN 2 2	FEB 1 1 '10	
JA 19 '05	FEB 2 5 '08	MAR 0 1 '10	
OC 25	MAR 2 7 '08	MAR 1 6 '10	
FE 18 '05	APR 0 8 '08	MAR 2 5 '10	
MR 18 05	MAY 0 6	OL 1 8	
AP 06 '05	MAY 1 5	APR 1 9 '10	
OC 20	JAN 2 0 '09	V 0 4 '10	
AP 19 '07	MAR 0 2 '09	OCT 0 4 '11	

Top 10 Football Sackers

Jeff Savage
AR B.L.: 5.7
Points: 1.0   MG

TOP 10 FOOTBALL SACKERS

Jeff Savage

SPORTS TOP 10

Enslow Publishers, Inc.

44 Fadem Road	PO Box 38
Box 699	Aldershot
Springfield, NJ 07081	Hants GU12 6BP
USA	UK

Library of Congress Cataloging-in-Publication Data

Savage, Jeff.
      Top 10 football sackers / by Jeff Savage.
          p. cm.—(Sports top 10)
      Includes bibliographical references (p.) and index.
      ISBN 0-89490-805-7
         1. Football players—United States—Biography—Juvenile
literature. 2. Football—Defense—Juvenile literature.
[1. Football players.] I. Title. II Series.
GV939.A1S28 1997
796.332'092—dc20
  [B]   96-25339
                                             CIP
                                           AC

Printed in the United States of America

10 9 8 7 6 5 4 3 2 1

Photo Credits: "© Dave Boss/NFLP", p. 14; Dallas Cowboys Football Club, pp. 10, 13, 25; "© Malcolm Emmons/NFL Photos" pp. 17, 22, 33; Michael F. Fabus, Team Photographer, Pittsburgh Steelers, pp. 7, 9; Photo by Dave Gaddis, Seattle Seahawks, p. 21; Green Bay Packers, pp. 38, 41; The Indianapolis Colts, pp. 26, 29; Photographer Jerry Pinkhus, New York Football Giants, pp. 35, 37; St. Louis Rams, pp. 42, 45; Corky Trewin, Photographer, Seattle Seahawks, p. 19; Tom West, Minnesota Vikings, Public Relations, p. 30.

Cover Photo: Green Bay Packers.

Interior Design: Richard Stalzer.

CONTENTS

INTRODUCTION

THE QUARTERBACK DROPS BACK TO pass. He stands in the pocket and looks downfield. All of a sudden—bam!—he goes down like a sack of potatoes. A sack!

What is a sack?

When a defensive tackle bull-rushes through the middle, lowers his shoulder, and plants the quarterback into the turf—that's a sack. When a defensive end makes a swim move on his blocker, grabs the quarterback by the jersey with one hand, and flings him to the ground—that's a sack. When a linebacker speeds around the outside, heads straight for the quarterback, and drills him from the blind side—that's a sack.

A sack can stop a drive, put a team out of field goal range, or cause a fumble. A sack can win a football game.

Quarterback Fran Tarkenton holds many all-time passing records. A record Fran is not proud to own is *"most times sacked."* Fran was tackled behind the line of scrimmage 483 times in his career. Phil Simms is second all-time, getting sacked 477 times. Warren Moon was once sacked 12 times in a game. So was Bert Jones. All National Football League quarterbacks know the painful feeling of getting sacked.

Who does the sacking?

The sack artists.

Sackers are defensive players with one primary goal—getting to the quarterback.

Sacks were long overlooked in the NFL. In fact, the league didn't recognize sacks as an official statistic until 1982. Before then, the league recorded sacks simply as "yards lost attempting to pass." No credit was given to the defensive player.

Researchers have viewed old game films to compile a

true list of all-time sackers. The NFL still does not recognize sacks prior to 1982 as official.

According to league statistics, Deacon Jones has one extra point—and no sacks. In truth, Deacon is the all-time sacks leader, with 189.5 sacks. (A half sack is recorded when two players sack the quarterback at the same time.) Jones even coined the term "sack."

"When a defensive lineman dominates the line of scrimmage," says Deacon, "he can totally control the game. I did it."[1]

We've searched every decade of pro football history to find the ten best sackers of all time. Some have retired. Some are still playing. Certainly there are many more great sackers. Perhaps you can think of others. In the meantime, here is *our* list.

CAREER STATISTICS

Sacker	Position	Years Played	Sacks
MEAN JOE GREENE	DT	1969-1981	74
CHARLES HALEY	OLB-DE	1986-	96.5
DEACON JONES	DE	1961-1974	189.5
CORTEZ KENNEDY	DT	1990-	38.5
BOB LILLY	DT-DE	1961-1974	89
GINO MARCHETTI	DE	1952-1966	73
ALAN PAGE	DT-DE	1967-1981	148.5
LAWRENCE TAYLOR	OLB	1981-1993	142
REGGIE WHITE	DE	1985-	157.5
JACK YOUNGBLOOD	DE	1971-1984	150.5

MEAN JOE GREENE

MEAN JOE GREENE HATED LOSING. His Pittsburgh Steelers were getting beat in Philadelphia by the Eagles. The year was 1970. In Greene's rookie season a year earlier, the Steelers had won just one game.

Greene thought he was being held on every play. The referees weren't calling it. Finally, before the Eagle center could snap the football for another play, Greene walked over, grabbed the ball, and threw it into the second deck of the stands. Then he stomped off the field.

The players couldn't believe what they saw. "We watched the ball spiral into the seats. It seemed like it took forever. The crowd was dead silent," remembers Steeler linebacker Andy Russell. "And the players—there we were, we didn't have a ball, we didn't have a left tackle. It was like Joe was saying, 'O.K., if you won't play right, we won't play at all.' Nobody else would do such a thing."[1]

Mean Joe Greene was unique. Greene was the first building block in Pittsburgh's dynasty of the 1970s. He was a six-foot four-inch, 260-pound lineman from North Texas State who manhandled offensive linemen in college. Greene got his nickname because North Texas State was called the Mean Green Machine. He was gentle off the field; he was a terror on it.

Greene proved to the Steelers how mean he really was. He once shattered four of Cleveland Browns guard Bob DeMarco's teeth. He tried to twist the head off an opponent who was holding him. He stomped on the head of another after getting clipped. He spit on Chicago Bears tough-guy linebacker Dick Butkus in front of everybody. He routinely

MEAN JOE GREENE

Making his presence felt, Greene is closing in on Dolphins' quarterback Bob Griese. Greene was the leader of the Steel Curtain defense that led the Steelers to four Super Bowl championships in the 1970s.

insulted opponents at the line of scrimmage. One time, he stole the ball from a quarterback, thundered into the end zone with it, tossed it over his head, caught it behind his back, and handed it to a cheerleader.

Charles Edward Greene was born September 24, 1946. He grew up in Temple, Texas, without a father. His mother liked to call him Joe. As a boy, he chopped and picked cotton in the fields. In the eighth grade, he weighed 158 pounds. The football coach claimed Joe was too clumsy and wasn't good enough to get a full uniform. He quit.

Joe weighed 203 pounds as a freshman. He played middle linebacker as a sophomore, and got kicked out of every game. He got kicked out of nine more as a junior. "I ran over a few officials," Mean Joe later said, "sometimes intentionally."[2]

Greene developed into a great pass rusher in Pittsburgh. He was named All-Pro ten times, and was the NFL Defensive Player of the Year twice. He was the leader of the Steel Curtain defensive line, along with L. C. Greenwood, Ernie Holmes, and Dwight White, as the Steelers won four Super Bowls in the 1970s.

"Any edge I can get, I'll take," Greene admitted during his playing days. "I do play football no-holds-barred."[3]

MEAN JOE GREENE

BORN: September 24, 1946, Temple, Texas.

COLLEGE: North Texas State University.

PRO: Pittsburgh Steelers, 1969–1981.

HONORS: Pro Football Hall of Fame, 1987.

Using his incredible strength, Greene breaks through the line to deliver another devastating hit. His fierce style of play made him a ten time All-Pro selection.

CHARLES HALEY

Charles Haley has always been a winner. Haley has more Super Bowl rings than any other player.

CHARLES HALEY

THE LIMOUSINE PULLED ALONGSIDE THE curb at the Dallas airport. Cowboys owner Jerry Jones rolled down the window. He told the man holding the suitcase to get in. Charles Haley squeezed his six-foot-five-inch, 250-pound frame into the backseat, and together they rode off.

The Cowboys had just acquired Haley in a trade with the San Francisco 49ers. Jones wanted to greet the linebacker at the airport. "Charles, I know you're in Dallas now," Jones said, "but are you leaving your heart in San Francisco?"[1]

Haley did not utter a word. He leaned forward and glared at the owner. The message was clear.

Charles Haley came to Texas on that warm August evening in 1992 wearing two Super Bowl rings. No Dallas Cowboy had a ring.

Haley was a pass-rushing force who helped the 49ers win back-to-back Super Bowls in 1989 and 1990. In six years with the Niners, he played in three Pro Bowls, was named the team's most courageous and inspirational player, and spent much of his time harassing the opposing quarterback. His two sacks in Super Bowl XXIII kept the 49ers within striking distance of the Cincinnati Bengals, allowing Joe Montana to win the game with a touchdown pass in the dying seconds.

Haley also had trouble in San Francisco. His flamboyant style was too showy for some of the team's coaches. His boldness was too strong for some of the players. Many 49ers were glad to see Haley go.

The Cowboys were happy to have him. From his outside

linebacker position, Haley could streak to the quarterback like a comet. Instantly, the Dallas defense became top-ranked in the NFL.

Five months after Haley left the 49ers, he returned to San Francisco for the NFC Championship Game wearing a star on his helmet. Dallas won the game, then the Super Bowl, and Haley had his third ring. The next year was a repeat performance. Haley's strength, speed, agility, and production as a blitzing linebacker made the Dallas defense tops again. The Cowboys beat the 49ers in the NFC title game, won the Super Bowl again, and Haley was fitted for his fourth ring. Two years later, the Cowboys won the 1996 Super Bowl. Charles had his fifth ring. No other NFL player has won as many.

"Charles was the last piece of the puzzle Dallas needed," said 49ers center Bart Oates. "That outside pass rush he gives them is a trademark of their team."[2]

Charles was born January 6, 1964. He spent much of his young life working on a farm in Gladys, Virginia. His father had to work two jobs. Charles knew what it was like to be poor.

Now Charles knows about being rich. He signed a four-year, $12 million contract with the Cowboys in 1995. He has suffered from a recurring back problem in recent years, but he plans to terrorize quarterbacks for a long time to come.

"I can't imagine taking the field without Charles Haley," owner Jones said. "Without him, we couldn't spell Super Bowl."[3]

CHARLES HALEY

BORN: January 6, 1964, Campbell County, Virginia.

COLLEGE: James Madison University.

PRO: San Francisco 49ers, 1986–1991; Dallas Cowboys, 1992– .

RECORDS: Five Super Bowl rings.

Haley has made an enormous impact on the Dallas Cowboys' defense. After his arrival in Dallas in 1992, the Cowboys defense rose to No. 1 in the league.

DEACON JONES

Deacon Jones looks to finish the play. Although sacks prior to 1982 are not counted, Jones has had more sacks than anyone else with 189.5.

LOS ANGELES RAMS SCOUTS JOHNNY Sanders and Eddie Kotal played the film over and over again. They couldn't believe what they were seeing. The scouts had been watching film of a speedy college running back, but it seemed that on every play, the running back was run down from behind by the same huge lineman.

"This giant kept showing up on the film," Sanders said. "We kept saying out loud, Who is that guy? We knew we had to find out."[1]

The lineman's name was David Jones. He was born December 9, 1938, in Eatonville, Florida. He played football for little-known Mississippi Vocational College. The Rams drafted him in the fourteenth round of the 1961 draft. It turned out to be a great pick.

David Jones showed up at the Rams training camp as a six-foot-five-inch, 250-pound Goliath. He announced that his first name would no longer be David—it would be Deacon. He figured Deacon was more memorable.

Deacon Jones was memorable, indeed. No one was better at getting to the quarterback. He was so mobile that even two linemen had trouble containing him. He could chase down a quarterback with his speed.

How fast was Jones? One time, Washington Redskins swift receiver Bobby Mitchell caught a short pass and headed upfield. Jones turned and chased him. Jones quickly caught up with Mitchell, but instead of tackling him right away, Jones ran alongside Mitchell for ten yards, then made the tackle. Jones explained later that he just wanted to see if he was as fast as the speedy receiver. He was.

A year after he joined the Rams, Jones created the headslap. At the snap of the ball, Jones would rise up and clobber the blocker in front of him on the side of the helmet. "I had good hand-eye coordination. That's why I developed the headslap," Deacon recalls. "I could rat-a-tat-tat upside your head and make you dizzy, then blow past you and get to the quarterback."[2] The headslap is illegal today.

The Ram defensive line became known as the Fearsome Foursome, and featured Merlin Olsen as the other heavyweight pass rusher (several players filled the other two spots). Jones clearly was the leader of the feared line, though. Surrounded by reporters in the locker room one day in 1964, Jones referred to his tackling of the quarterback behind the line of scrimmage as a "sack." The name stuck.

NFL seasons were shorter in the 1960s. Teams played fourteen games, rather than today's sixteen-game schedule. There weren't as many opportunities to compile sacks. In 1967, for instance, Ram quarterbacks were sacked a total of 25 times. Fewer games didn't slow Jones. That same year, he recorded 26 sacks by himself.

After eleven years with the Rams, Jones played two years with the San Diego Chargers, and one with the Redskins, before retiring in 1974. In fourteen years, he compiled 189.5 sacks. He was named to the Pro Football Hall of Fame in 1980, his first year of eligibility.

Rams public relations director Rick Smith says simply, "Deacon Jones was a marvel. There may never be another pass rusher as great as he was."[3]

DEACON JONES

BORN: December 9, 1938, Eatonville, Florida.

COLLEGE: Mississippi Vocational College.

PRO: Los Angeles Rams, 1961–1971; San Diego Chargers, 1972–1973; Washington Redskins, 1974.

RECORDS: NFL, all-time sack leader (189.5).

HONORS: Pro Football Hall of Fame, 1980.

Deacon Jones looks to sack the Saints quarterback. Plays like this are the reason he was inducted into the Hall of Fame in 1980.

CORTEZ KENNEDY

THE SEATTLE SEAHAWKS' HOPES OF winning a football game were slim. It was 1992, Cortez Kennedy was in his third year, and most of his teammates were even newer.

The New England Patriots also were rebuilding. Kennedy knew the early season game at Foxboro Stadium in Massachusetts would be a rare chance for a victory. Kennedy took matters into his own hands.

The six-foot-one-inch, 320-pound defensive tackle used his enormous strength to roll like a human bowling ball through the Patriots' line. New England put six-foot-four-inch, 305-pound left guard Reggie Redding in front of Kennedy, and then double-teamed him with another lineman. It didn't matter. In the first half, Kennedy sacked quarterback Hugh Millen three times and caused him to fumble twice. The Patriots never crossed midfield.

"It was the most impressive first half I've ever seen," said Seahawks coach Tom Flores. "He played like a man possessed."[1]

Kennedy didn't stop there. He finished the game with 10 tackles, 5 for losses totaling 33 yards, and the Seahawks won, 10–6. "He's quick as heck," said Redding. "He went outside me a lot, and I couldn't do a thing about it."[2]

Cortez is known affectionately as Tez. With his large, round body, he also has been known at various times as Water Buffalo, Baby Cakes, Tons of Buns, Big Fella, and the Sofa. Kennedy says he doesn't mind the nicknames.

"I like being big because it gives me confidence," he says. "Nobody wants to mess with me."[3]

Why should they? Kennedy is as ferocious a defensive

CORTEZ KENNEDY

Scanning over the situation, Cortez Kennedy looks to make the stop. The Seahawks made Kennedy the third player selected in the 1990 NFL Draft.

tackle as pro football has ever had. He can lift offensive linemen and hurl them backward into the quarterback. He can leap over low, cutting blocks with his surprising quickness.

The Seahawks have struggled as a team, but Kennedy certainly gets noticed. Even when Seattle finished 2–14 in 1992, Kennedy was named the NFL Defensive Player of the Year.

"He can do it all," says Seahawks All-Pro safety Eugene Robinson. "He chases down screens from the back side, he slams quarterbacks. I could go on and on. He's got loads of talent just oozing out of that big body."[4]

Cortez Kennedy was born August 23, 1968. Growing up in Wilson, Arkansas, Cortez weighed 155 pounds in ninth grade, 219 in tenth, 235 in eleventh, and 275 in twelfth. He would come home in the afternoon, gobble up an entire package of hot dogs, then eat dinner an hour later.

He won a college national championship at the University of Miami, then was the third player picked in the 1990 NFL draft.

Kennedy works out on a Stairmaster machine every day to maintain his weight. "But don't forget," says Patriots coach Bill Parcells with a wink, "one of the greatest athletes of all time, Babe Ruth, was a little chunky."[5]

CORTEZ KENNEDY

BORN: August 23, 1968, Wilson, Arkansas.

COLLEGE: University of Miami.

PRO: Seattle Seahawks, 1990– .

HONORS: NFL Defensive Player of the Year, 1992.

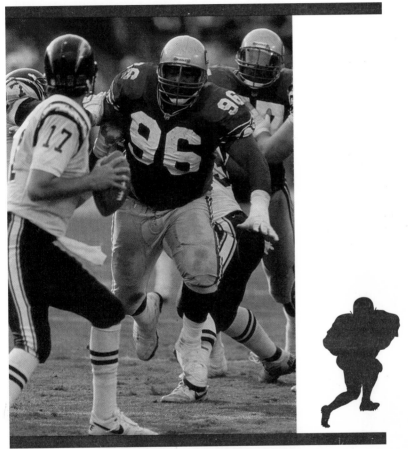

Breaking free of his blocker, Cortez Kennedy eyes his next sack victim. Kennedy was the Defensive Player of the Year in 1992.

BOB LILLY

Bob Lilly looks to stop the running back behind the line of scrimmage. Lilly was the first Cowboys' player to have his name placed in their Ring of Honor.

TEXAS CHRISTIAN UNIVERSITY FOOTBALL COACH Abe Martin was desperate for linemen in 1957. He remembered seeing a big boy named Robert Lilly play in a high school volleyball tournament in Throckmorton, Texas. Martin learned that the boy had moved away to Oregon with his family. The coach sent Lilly a letter, asking him to come to TCU. When the coach didn't hear back, he figured he had wasted a five-cent stamp.

Two months later, Lilly got his mother to pack him some sandwiches and lemonade, drove his 1947 Studebaker the 1,600 miles to Texas in 35 hours, and walked into Martin's office.

"You look a little skinny to me," the coach said.

"It was a hard trip," Lilly said with a smile.[1]

A star was born.

Robert Lilly was born July 26, 1939, in Olney, Texas. Now he had returned to his home state to play college football. Lilly became known as the Purple Cloud at TCU, because he hovered over opponents like a cloud in his purple uniform. He was unanimously voted an All-American defensive tackle. His knack for sacking the quarterback had pro scouts drooling. The newly formed Dallas Cowboys gobbled him up.

Lilly will always be the No.1 Dallas Cowboy. He was the team's first-ever official draft pick (1961), first defensive Pro Bowl selection (1962), first name in the Cowboys' Ring of Honor (1975), and the first who played his entire career with the Cowboys to be elected to the Hall of Fame (1980).

After Lilly's rookie year, coach Tom Landry said, "Lilly

has done very well for a first-year man. He could become one of the really good ones."[2]

Three years later, after another sorry season for the Cowboys, Landry said the lone bright spot on the team was Lilly. "He always broke his first block, always, and usually his second or third. There is no one man in football who can contain Lilly."[3]

Lilly endured the growing pains of a building team for many years. The Cowboys finally began winning in the late 1960s, and then reached the Super Bowl for the first time in the 1970 season. They lost on a last-second field goal, but vowed to return. They did the following year, and trounced the Miami Dolphins, 24–3, in Super Bowl VI. Before that game, Philadelphia coach Ed Khayat, whose Eagles had lost twice to Dallas that year, said, "When you're getting ready to play Dallas, you spend about half your time trying to figure out how you're going to play Bob Lilly."[4]

On one play in Super Bowl VI, Lilly broke through a triple-team to sack Dolphins quarterback Bob Griese for a huge 29-yard loss. Said Griese, "There isn't any use arguing with him if he gets hold of your jersey. You just fall wherever Bob wants."[5]

BOB LILLY

BORN: July 26, 1939, Olney, Texas.

COLLEGE: Texas Christian University.

PRO: Dallas Cowboys, 1961–1974.

HONORS: First-ever Cowboy All-Pro. Pro Football Hall of Fame, 1980.

Bob Lilly was the Cowboys' first-ever draft pick. He played his entire career with Dallas and was elected into the Hall of Fame in 1980.

GINO MARCHETTI

Gino Marchetti was feared by opposing quarterbacks. He would have appeared in eleven straight Pro-Bowls had he not injured his ankle in the 1958 championship game making a game-saving tackle.

GINO MARCHETTI WAS KNOWN FOR his great pass-rushing skills. The biggest play of his life, however, was a tackle after a 2-yard gain. Marchetti's Baltimore Colts trailed the New York Giants, 17–14, in the 1958 NFL Championship Game. With two minutes left, the Giants faced a crucial third-and-three situation near midfield. If they made the first down, they could run out the clock.

Giants quarterback Charley Conerly handed the ball to running back Frank Gifford. Marchetti pushed the entire right side of the Giant offensive line backward. Gifford was forced outside. Marchetti chased the running back, wrapped him up, and slammed him to the turf. Defensive teammate Big Daddy Lipscomb arrived a moment later, and his 300-pound bulk landed squarely on Marchetti's ankle, breaking it.

Gifford was six inches short of the first down. Marchetti was carried off the field on a stretcher, but he refused to leave the sideline until the game ended. The Colts took possession, drove for the tying field goal, then won in overtime, in what many consider the greatest pro football game ever played. In the locker room afterward, Marchetti's teammates presented him with the game ball.

Gino Marchetti was born January 2, 1927, in Smithers, West Virginia. There was little hint of Gino's football ability as a boy. His Italian immigrant family urged him not to participate in such a rough sport. Gino convinced his parents to let him play his senior year of high school. As a lineman, Gino was named the team's Most Valuable Player at Antioch High School in California.

A year later, Gino was in the U.S. Army, fighting in the pivotal Battle of the Bulge in World War II.

After the war, Marchetti played at Modesto Junior College and at the University of San Francisco, where he developed into the best college tackle on the Pacific Coast. The New York Yanks drafted him in 1952, but within a year, they became the Dallas Texans, and then folded. Gino joined the Baltimore Colts, and became universally feared by opposing quarterbacks.

Legendary coach George Allen says Marchetti was the best defensive lineman he ever coached against. "Gino just overpowered blockers and blasted in on the passer," Allen says, "and when he got to the quarterback he really pounded the guy. Marchetti usually gave him an extra lick, too. To be honest about it, Gino wasn't the cleanest player ever."[1]

Marchetti would have owned a record streak of eleven consecutive Pro Bowls, if it had not been for Big Daddy Lipscomb's falling on his ankle. As it was, in 1969, the Pro Football Hall of Fame Board of Selectors named Marchetti the finest defensive end in the NFL's first fifty years. In 1995, he was elected to the seventy-fifth Anniversary All-Time Team.

GINO MARCHETTI

BORN: January 2, 1927, Smithers, West Virginia.
COLLEGE: University of San Francisco.
PRO: Dallas Texans, 1952; Baltimore Colts, 1953–1964, 1966.
HONORS: Pro Football Hall of Fame, 1972.

Gino is considered by many to be one of the best defensive linemen to have ever played. In 1995, he was elected to the NFL's 75th Anniversary All-Time Team.

ALAN PAGE

Leaping high into the air, Alan Page attempts to block the pass. Alan Page joined the Minnesota Vikings as their No. 1 draft choice in 1967.

THE FIELD AT METROPOLITAN STADIUM in Bloomington, Minnesota, was frozen solid. The temperature was below zero. The Los Angeles Rams were locked in a bitter playoff battle with the Minnesota Vikings.

Rams quarterback Roman Gabriel dropped back to pass. Tom Mack, the Ram All-Pro guard, blocked Viking defensive tackle Alan Page to the ground. Gabriel threw a pass over the middle. As the ball was soaring above his head, Page leaped to his feet, jumped in the air, and intercepted it. Players on both sides couldn't believe such an acrobatic play could be made, especially in the snow. The Vikings cashed in with a touchdown and won the game.

Alan Page played with tremendous intelligence and desire. No other lineman in history can match the wide range of Page's statistical achievements.

Page first gained fame as an All-American lineman on Notre Dame's 1966 national championship team. He joined the NFL as the Vikings' No. 1 draft pick in 1967. He earned the starting right defensive tackle position in the fourth game of his rookie year.

In his fifteen-year career, Page never missed a game. In 238 games, he amassed these numbers: 24 fumble recoveries, 28 blocked kicks, 148.5 sacks, and 1,431 tackles.

Page led a Minnesota front four known as the Purple People Eaters. The other members were Carl Eller, Jim Marshall, and Gary Larsen, but it was Page who rushed the quarterback with a reckless abandon. "A defensive player should think of himself more as an aggressor, not as a defender," Page said once. "Don't sit back and wait to react to what the offense does. If you are going to make a mistake, make it aggressively."[1]

After the 1971 season, Page became the first defensive player to be named NFL Most Valuable Player. He was NFC Defensive Player of the Year four other times. In an eleven-year span with Page, the Vikings marched to 10 division titles and 4 Super Bowls.

Then, six games into the 1978 season, Page and the Vikings abruptly parted company. Page had embarked on an extensive running program that improved his speed and agility but reduced his playing weight fifteen pounds to 225 pounds. Vikings coach Bud Grant considered Page too light to play. "I talked to Alan about his running, but he remained firm in his position," said Grant, who cut Page from the team.[2]

Within hours, Page was claimed off waivers by the Chicago Bears and named a starter. He led the Bears in sacks that year, played three more stellar seasons for Chicago, and retired in 1981, after recording 3.5 sacks in his final game.

Page attended law school in the off-season during his last few years in the league. He currently serves as an Associate Justice of the Minnesota Supreme Court.

Alan Page was born August 7, 1945. He grew up in Canton, Ohio, in the shadow of the Pro Football Hall of Fame. In 1988, he proudly became the first Canton native to enter the Hall.

ALAN PAGE

BORN: August 7, 1945, Canton, Ohio.

COLLEGE: University of Notre Dame.

PRO: Minnesota Vikings, 1967–1978; Chicago Bears, 1978–1981.

HONORS: NFL Most Valuable Player, 1971; Pro Football Hall of Fame, 1988.

Ready to react, Alan Page looks for the man with the ball. In 1971, Page became the first defensive player to be named NFL Most Valuable Player.

LAWRENCE TAYLOR

HE IS KNOWN SIMPLY AS "LT." The impact he made on the NFL may be unmatched.

"Lawrence Taylor changed the way defense is played, the way pass-rushing is played, the way linebackers play, and the way offenses block linebackers," says NFL analyst John Madden.[1]

Lawrence Taylor was born February 4, 1959, in Williamsburg, Virginia. He was a high school football star, then became an All-American linebacker at the University of North Carolina. The New York Giants reached for him with the second pick of the 1981 draft. The Giants were a sorry organization. They had had just two winning seasons in the previous seventeen years, and hadn't been to the playoffs since 1963.

When Taylor arrived at training camp, he announced that he would turn things around for the Giants. In the team's first camp scrimmage, he showed how. He registered 4 sacks and a fumble recovery.

At his first press conference at Giants Stadium, Taylor declared, "I like to eat quarterbacks in the backfield."[2] Reporters saw what he meant. In his first-ever preseason game, Taylor recorded 10 solo tackles, 2 sacks, and a fumble recovery.

When LT was finished thirteen years later, he had equaled an NFL record by appearing in ten consecutive Pro Bowls, as well as in two Super Bowls. Along the way, he was the NFL Rookie of the Year in 1981, the NFL Most Valuable Player in 1986 (the second defensive player so honored), and a unanimous choice to the NFL's All-1980s team.

LAWRENCE TAYLOR

Running full stride, Taylor is in hot pursuit of an opposing player. Many consider Taylor to be the best linebacker of all time.

Taylor redefined the art of pass-rushing. His specialty was to line up outside and make a speed rush around the linemen. Sometimes he would merely jump over them. Opponents had to ask before each play, "Where's LT?"

"There comes a time in a game when you know a key play is coming up," Taylor once said. "You can just feel it in the air."[3]

Taylor probably made more great plays than any other linebacker in history. His nickname was Superman.

Often, he played a starring role while injured. There was the time in 1989 when San Francisco 49er tight end Wesley Walls took LT down on a cut block and broke his ankle. Taylor played the next week, anyway.

Then there was the big Sunday night game in 1988 against the New Orleans Saints when half the New York defense was out. Taylor was in terrible pain with a torn deltoid muscle, and he kept stripping off his shirt on the sideline to adjust his shoulder pads. He registered 10 tackles, got 2 sacks, and forced 2 fumbles, and the Giants won by a field goal. "After the game," coach Bill Parcells recalls, "I went over to LT, and we touched foreheads. He knew and I knew, but no one else knew what he had gone through."[4]

In 1993, Superman hung up his cape and said, "I've been able to do things in this game that haven't been done before."[5]

LAWRENCE TAYLOR

BORN: February 4, 1959, Williamsburg, Virginia.

COLLEGE: University of North Carolina.

PRO: New York Giants, 1981–1993.

HONORS: NFL Most Valuable Player, 1986.

Fully extended, Lawrence Taylor wraps up the opposing quarterback. In 1981, Taylor was named NFL Rookie of the Year.

REGGIE WHITE

Using both force and determination, Reggie White is trying to escape from his blocker. White is listed as having the most sacks in NFL history, though sacks prior to 1982 are not counted.

THE CONTRACT WAS SIGNED—FOUR years, $17 million. Reggie White was the richest defensive player in NFL history. Now it was time to play.

White was introduced as a Green Bay Packer for the 1993 season opener, and Lambeau Field in eastern Wisconsin shook from the thunderous cheers of thousands of fans. On the opposite sideline stood White's old team-mates—the Philadelphia Eagles.

The Eagles knew White had one thing on his mind— sack. Still, they couldn't stop him. On the Eagles' first possession, White slashed between the guard and tackle, caught quarterback Randall Cunningham from behind, and stripped the ball from him. The Packers recovered. Later in the first quarter, White ran over two blockers, smashed his shoulder into Cunningham, and jarred the ball loose. The Packers recovered.

It went like this all day long. White kept making big plays. Even though the Eagles rallied to win by a field goal, all the praise afterward was for White. "Reggie," Cunningham simply said, "was all business."[1]

Reggie White was born December 19, 1961. As a boy growing up in Chattanooga, Tennessee, Reggie was called Bigfoot because he was big for his age, with large feet. When he was twelve, he told his mother he wanted to be two things—a pro football player and a minister.

Reggie has met both his childhood goals. In addition to playing football, he is an ordained Baptist minister. His football nickname is Minister of Defense. He contributes thousands of dollars each year to organizations that fight the evils of society, from drug and alcohol abuse, to the absence of role models. "People say, 'Where are all the role models?'" White says. "Well, I want to be a role model. I want kids to look up to me."[2]

This is not hard to do. White is a rare blend of speed, power, and desire. In his first ten years in the NFL, White never missed a game due to injury. According to official league statistics, he is the all-time sacks leader with 143 drops in 153 games. Sacks were not counted prior to 1982, of course. Unofficially, Deacon Jones is nearly forty sacks ahead of anyone else, but White may catch up to him yet.

The praise for Reggie tells the story:

"He's the best sacker I've ever been around," said former Arizona Cardinals coach Buddy Ryan.[3]

"If there's a better sacker," said former Chicago Bears coach Mike Ditka, "I haven't seen him."[4]

White is outgoing and funny. He likes to clown around in the locker room, doing impressions of Elvis Presley or Rodney Dangerfield. On the field, though, crouched in his stance, ready to rush the quarterback, he is all business. Just ask Randall Cunningham.

REGGIE WHITE

BORN: December 19, 1961, Chattanooga, Tennessee.

COLLEGE: University of Tennessee.

PRO: Philadelphia Eagles, 1985–1992; Green Bay Packers, 1993– .

HONORS: NFL Seventy-Five-Year All-Anniversary Team.

Reggie White takes a well deserved rest. Besides being a great football star, White is also an ordained Baptist minister.

JACK YOUNGBLOOD

Although considered to be small for a defensive end, Youngblood was able to become an All-Pro player.

JACK YOUNGBLOOD

JACK YOUNGBLOOD HOBBLED OFF THE field. Around him, more than 103,000 people were filing out of the Rose Bowl in Pasadena, California. Super Bowl XIV had just ended. Youngblood's Los Angeles Rams had lost.

In the locker room afterward, with dozens of reporters and players milling about, Youngblood quietly slipped into the trainer's room for an X-ray. His left leg was broken. It had been fractured for two weeks.

"Is your leg any worse than it was before the game?" a reporter asked Youngblood when he emerged from the trainer's room.

"I don't know," he answered softly. "It hurts right now, I know that."[1]

Youngblood had suffered the injury in the third quarter of a playoff game against the Dallas Cowboys. He played the rest of the game, anyway. Then, knowing his leg was broken, he insisted on playing a week later in the NFC title game against the Tampa Bay Buccaneers. He led the Rams to a 9-0 shutout and their first-ever Super Bowl. Then, he played the entire Super Bowl, sometimes limping back to the huddle. A day later, doctors put his leg in a cast.

Youngblood was small as defensive ends go, weighing just 240 pounds most of his career. He wasn't especially fast, either. What made Jack Youngblood great was his will to succeed. "He's as competitive a man as I've ever come across," said Rams coach John Robinson.[2]

Jack Youngblood was born January 26, 1950, in Jacksonville, Florida. He grew up in nearby Monticello and never gave much thought to football. "My heroes were bird dogs," he says. "Hunting and fishing was my world."[3]

Jack played prep football at tiny Jefferson County High School, but his skills weren't polished, and major college scouts never saw him play. He never got a phone call from a recruiter.

The struggling football program at the University of Florida was in need of linemen. The Gators took a chance on the country boy, and it paid off. Youngblood developed into an All-American defensive end.

In February 1971, the Rams drafted him in the first round. He studied under the great Deacon Jones for a year until Deacon left the Rams for San Diego. The next year, Youngblood shared the left defensive end position with Fred Dryer. In 1973, Dryer moved to the right side, and Youngblood took over the position. One season later, he was an All-Pro.

For the next decade, quarterbacks everywhere feared Youngblood. As they dropped back to pass, they could feel his presence. "Roger Staubach has a feel of where I am, all the time," Youngblood explained once. "So does Fran Tarkenton. Fran will look to see where I am before he throws the football."[4]

When Youngblood retired, he unofficially ranked second all-time in sacks behind his mentor, Deacon Jones. Quarterbacks around the NFL, who had long been hunted by Youngblood, were happy to see him go back to hunting birds.

JACK YOUNGBLOOD

BORN: January 26, 1950, Jacksonville, Florida.

COLLEGE: University of Florida.

PRO: Los Angeles Rams, 1971–1984.

RECORDS: Played in 201 consecutive games for Rams.

With the quarterback firm in his grasp, Jack Youngblood has a sack. Jack is so determined to do all that he can, he once played in the Super Bowl with a broken leg.

Chapter Notes

Introduction

    1. John Turney, "Deacon Speaks," *College & Pro Football Newsweekly*, October 31, 1994, p. 15.

Mean Joe Greene

    1. George Allen, *Pro Football's 100 Greatest Players* (Indianapolis: The Bobbs-Merrill Company, Inc., 1982), p. 154.

    2. Roy Blount, Jr., "He Does What He Wants Out There," *Sports Illustrated*, September 5, 1994, p. 147.

    3. Ibid., p. 138.

Charles Haley

    1. Thomas George, "Cowboy With Angry Score to Settle," *The New York Times*, January 13, 1993, p. 87.

    2. Mike Baldwin, "Frisco's Loss Is Dallas' Gain," *Daily Oklahoman*, January 14, 1995, p. 15.

    3. Ed Werder, "Haley Gets $12 Million Deal," *Dallas Morning News*, July 11, 1995, p. 4.

Deacon Jones

    1. Personal interview with Johnny Sanders, August 21, 1985.

    2. Personal interview with Deacon Jones, June 30, 1995.

    3. Personal interview with Rick Smith, July 1, 1995.

Cortez Kennedy

    1. Jill Lieber, "The NFL's Premier Defensive Tackle," *Sports Illustrated*, November 30, 1992, p. 49.

    2. Ibid.

    3. Ibid.

    4. Dan Dieffenbach, "A Quarterback's Nightmare," *Sport*, October 1994, p. 68.

    5. Paul Attner, "The Young and the Gifted," *The Sporting News*, October 4, 1993, p. 36.

Bob Lilly

    1. Gary Cartwright, "Bob Lilly, Defensive Tackle," *Sport*, October 1965, p. 16.

    2. Bob Beebe, "Lilly, No. 1 Draft Choice, Plays Large Role in Dallas Defense," *Minneapolis Star*, October 6, 1961, p. 1.

3. Cartwright, p. 37.

4. Tex Maule, "A Cowboy Stampede," *Sports Illustrated*, January 24, 1972, p. 14.

5. Pro Football Hall of Fame media guide, class of 1980.

Gino Marchetti

1. George Allen, *Pro Football's 100 Greatest Players* (Indianapolis: The Bobbs-Merrill Company, Inc., 1982), p. 132.

Alan Page

1. "Amazing Americans—Alan Page," (Special Advertising Feature) *Sports Illustrated*, May 18, 1992, p. 58.

2. Cooper Rollow, "Foursome Stakes Claim to Fame," *The Sporting News*, August 8, 1988, p. 37.

Lawrence Taylor

1. Craig Ellenport, "The Defense Rests," *Sport*, January 1993, p. 48.

2. Ibid, p. 49.

3. Paul Zimmerman, "LT on LT," *Sports Illustrated*, September 16, 1991, p. 48.

4. Ibid.

5. Staff editors, "Lawrence Taylor's Career Comes to Close With Loss," *Jet*, February 14, 1994, p. 50.

Reggie White

1. Peter King, "Painful Reunion," *Sports Illustrated*, September 20, 1993, p. 20.

2. Phil Anastasia, "Eagles; R&R Combo a Study in Contrasts," *The Sporting News*, October 9, 1989, p. 10.

3. Ibid.

4. Ibid.

Jack Youngblood

1. Dave Anderson, "We Had 'Em on the Ropes," *The New York Times*, January 21, 1980, p. C10.

2. Orlando Predators media guide.

3. Jack Smith, "The Hunting Season," *Los Angeles Times*, April 9, 1978, p. 11.

4. Ibid, p. 15.

INDEX